W9-CRP-871

The Value of Money

WHAT IS MONEY?

PORTIA SUMMERS

Enslow Publishing
101 W. 23rd Street
Suite 240
New York, NY 10011
USA

enslow.com

WORDS TO KNOW

bills–Money made from paper and cloth.

coins–Money made from pieces of metal.

currency–The money a particular country uses.

dollar–The American currency.

face–The front of a bill or coin.

goods–Products that are useful to a person as they are, such as food, paper, or clothing.

services–Something that a person is paid to do for others, such as washing their car, cutting their grass, or delivering their newspaper.

value–How much something is worth.

CONTENTS

A QUICK LOOK AT MONEY

penny   nickel   dime   quarter   half-dollar   one-dollar coin

1¢   5¢   10¢   25¢   50¢ $1

one-dollar bill
$1

five-dollar bill
$5

ten-dollar bill
$10

twenty-dollar bill
$20

WHAT IS MONEY?

Coins and bills are types of money, or currency. Coins are made from metal like copper, nickel, and silver.

Bills are not actually made from paper. They are made from 75% cotton and 25% linen and silk.

HOW DO YOU USE MONEY

People use money to pay for goods and services. Goods include things like food, clothes, electronics, or toys. Services include when your server brings your food at a restaurant, a haircut, or the plumber coming to fix the pipes at your house.

WHAT ARE COINS?

A penny is worth one cent. Its value is written as $0.01 or 1¢.

President Abraham Lincoln is on the front, or face, of the coin. The Lincoln Memorial in Washington, DC, is on the back.

Moments in Minting

The US one-dollar bill has many nicknames: greenback (because it is green in color), Washington (after the president on it), clam, and single. One common nickname is "buck." This is because before bills were in regular circulation, people bartered, or traded, deer skins.

A nickel is worth five cents, or 5¢, or $0.05.
President Thomas Jefferson is on the front of the nickel.
His house in Virginia, Monticello, is on the back.

A dime is worth ten cents, or 10¢, or $0.10.

President Franklin Delano Roosevelt (FDR) is on the face of the dime. The back has three symbols of the United States: the olive branch (for peace), the torch (for liberty), and the oak branch (for strength).

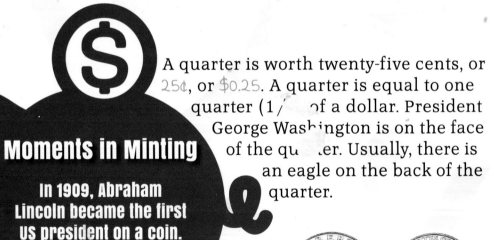

Moments in Minting

In 1909, Abraham Lincoln became the first US president on a coin.

A quarter is worth twenty-five cents, or 25¢, or $0.25. A quarter is equal to one quarter (1/) of a dollar. President George Washington is on the face of the quarter. Usually, there is an eagle on the back of the quarter.

But there is also a specially designed quarter for each of the 50 states.

Here's one for Louisiana.

There are also golden dollar coins. These are worth $1.00 each.

Some have Sacagawea (who helped famous explorers map the western part of the United States). Others have the Statue of Liberty on their face.

WHAT ARE BILLS?

A one-dollar bill is worth one dollar, written $1.00. One dollar equals 100 cents. President George Washington is on the front of the one-dollar bill.

A five-dollar bill is worth $5.00. President Abraham Lincoln is on the front of the five-dollar bill. The Lincoln Memorial is also on the back of the five-dollar bill, just like the penny.

Moments in Minting

The number 1 is written on the dollar bill eight times! Can you find all eight?

A ten-dollar bill is worth ten dollars, or $10.00. Alexander Hamilton, the first secretary of the treasury, is on the ten-dollar bill. But in 2015, it was announced that a famous woman in American history would replace him soon.

The twenty-dollar bill is worth $20.00. President Andrew Jackson is on the front of the bill.

On the back of the twenty-dollar bill is the White House.

There are higher bills, as well. President Ulysses S. Grant is on the fifty-dollar bill ($50), and Benjamin Franklin is on the one-hundred dollar bill ($100).

COMMON CURRENCY COMBINATIONS

Five pennies are worth 5¢.
A nickel is worth 5¢.
5 pennies = a nickel.

The Bureau of Engraving and Printing uses 9.7 tons of ink per day!

One quarter is worth 25¢. Four quarters are worth 100 cents.

100 cents equals one dollar. 4 quarters = $1.00

A five-dollar bill is worth $5.

Four five-dollar bills are worth $20.00.
A twenty-dollar bill is worth $20.00.

Four five-dollar bills have the same value as a twenty-dollar bill.

LEARN MORE

BOOKS

American Education Publishing. *The Complete Book of Time and Money, Grades K-3*. Greensboro, NC: 2009.

Furgang, Kathy. *National Geographic Kids: Everything Money: A Wealth of Facts, Photos, and Fun*. Washington, D.C.: National Geographic Children's Books, 2013.

Sieber, Arlyn G. *A Kid's Guide to Collecting Coins*. Fairfield, OH.: Krause Publications, 2011.

WEBSITES

H.I.P. Pocket Change

www.usmint.gov/kids

The official website of the United States Mint for kids!

Science Kids

www.sciencekids.co.nz/sciencefacts/technology/money.html

Read fun facts about money and currency!

INDEX

Published in 2017 by Enslow Publishing, LLC.
101 W. 23rd Street, Suite 240, New York, NY 10011

Library of Congress Cataloging-in-Publication Data
Names: Summers, Portia, author.
Title: What is money? / Portia Summers.
Description: New York, NY : Enslow Publishing, [2017] | Series: The value of money | Includes bibliographical references and index.
Identifiers: LCCN 2015045461| ISBN 9780766077188 (library bound) | ISBN 9780766077157 (pbk.) | ISBN 9780766077164 (6-pack)
Subjects: LCSH: Money--Juvenile literature.
Classification: LCC HG221.5 .S86 2016 | DDC 332.4--dc23
LC record available at http://lccn.loc.gov/2015045461

Printed in Malaysia

To Our Readers: We have done our best to make sure all website addresses in this book were active and appropriate when we went to press. However, the author and the publisher have no control over and assume no liability for the material available on those websites or on any websites they may link to. Any comments or suggestions can be sent by e-mail to customerservice@enslow.com.

Portions of this book originally appeared in the book *I Can Name Bills and Coins* by Rebecca Wingard-Nelson.

Photo Credits: Cover (green dollar sign background, used throughout the book) Rachael Arnott/Shutterstock.com, Fedorov Oleksiy/Shutterstock.com; (white dollar sign background, used throughout the book) Golden Shrimp/Shutterstock.com; VIGE. COM/Shutterstock.com (piggy bank with dollar sign, used throughout book); Golden Shrimp/Shutterstock.com (green cross pattern border, used throughout book); p. 2 Fadyukhin/iStockphoto. com; p. 3 AVprophoto/Shutterstock.com; p. 4 penny (used throughout the book), mattesimages/Shutterstock.com; nickel (used throughout the book), United States Mint image; dime and quarter (used throughout the book), B Brown/Shutterstock.com; half-dollar, Daniel D Malone/Shutterstock.com; one-dollar coin, JordiDelgado/ iStockphoto.com; one-dollar, five-dollar and twenty-dollar bills (used throughout the book) Anton_Ivanov/Shutterstock.com; ten-dollar bill, Pavel Kirichenko/Shutterstock.com; pp. 5 FrameAngel/ Shutterstock.com (coins), georged/Shutterstock.com (bills), ; p. 6 MagMos/iStockphoto.com; p. 7 Christopher David Howells/ Shutterstock.com; p. 8 Dennis W. Donohue/Shutterstock.com; p. 9 Oksana Mizina/Shutterstock.com; p. 11 d8nn/Shutterstock.com p. 12 gnoparus/Shutterstock.com; peterspiro/iStockphoto.com; p. 14 JGI/Jamie Grill/Blend Images/Getty Images; p. 16 Velishchuk Yevhen/Shutterstock.com; p.17 Ethel Wolvovitz/Alamy Stock Photo; p. 18 Peter Gridley/Stockbyte/Getty Images; p. 19 holbox/ Shutterstock.com; p. 20 OLJ Studio/Shutterstock.com; p. 22 szefei/ iStock/Thinkstock.com.